TAIJUTSU

Ninja Art of Unarmed Combat

By Charles Daniel

Disclaimer

Please note that the publisher of this instructional book is NOT RESPONSIBLE in any manner whatsoever for any injury which may occur by reading and/or following the instructions herein.

It is essential that before following any of the activities, physical or otherwise, herein described, the reader or readers should first consult his or her physician for advice on whether or not the reader or readers should embark on the physical activity described herein. Since the physical activities described herein may be too sophisticated in nature, it is essential that a physician be consulted.

Unique Publications
4201 Vanowen Place
Burbank, CA 91505

ISBN: 0-86568-085-X
Library of Congress Catalog Number: 86-051212

Designer: Danilo J. Silverio
Editor: Russell Maynard

Dedication

For Niki; may you live in a world where borders are not barriers, where weapons are instruments of enlightenment and not destruction, and where people's differences are sources of interest and acceptance rather than sources of misunderstanding and senseless conflict.

I would like to thank Dr. Masaaki Hatsumi and his Master teachers for their time and patience. Also, my thanks to Russell Maynard, who served as my training partner in the technique sequences, and to Ed Ikuta, who photographed the book.

Charles Daniel
August 10, 1986

About the Author

Charles Daniel is uniquely qualified to present the skills of taijutsu, the unarmed combat system of the ninja. He is a skilled martial artist, currently testing for his 5th degree black belt in ninjutsu with Dr. Hatsumi, and a well-known writer, including many articles for magazines and a book entitled, "Traditional Ninja Weapons."

Mr. Daniel welcomes correspondence from those interested in all martial arts and ninjutsu in particular. His American address is: P.O. Box 956933, Duluth, GA 30136. His European address is: Waxensteinstr 36, 8100 Garmish-Partenkirchen, W. Germany.

Introduction

This book is the author's attempt to present what is probably the most important aspect of ninjutsu in print. Of course, philosophy is very important to the ninja, but since technique is a reflection of philosophy, careful study of this book should shed some light on the ideas that were used, and are still followed today, by the "Shadow Warrior."

This book is, in many ways, a companion work to the author's "Traditional Ninja Weapons." However, the present work presents many new ideas about ninjutsu, which hopefully will help the reader gain a fuller understanding of this fascinating, albeit often misunderstood, martial art.

It should be noted that a complete presentation of taijutsu in one book is not possible. Any omissions made by the author should be taken as a reflection of what he thought important and may not necessarily be the opinion held by other ninjutsu instructors. Such differences are often caused when different instructors apply their martial arts for different reasons; a military instructor's techniques would be somewhat different from a policeman's techniques, and a woman's techniques would be even something else.

In this work, the author has outlined a general overview of taijutsu while remaining as true as possible to the art's traditional form. There are, of course, many special cases that have not been included in the book because of space considerations.

As always, the author would like to extend his thanks to the many instructors and training partners that have made this book possible.

Contents

Part I

Taijutsu

The ninja's close-combat system is called "taijutsu." Taijutsu translates into English as "body method." However, for the sake of general usage, taijutsu refers to the ninja's method of unarmed technique. As a method of unarmed self-defense, taijutsu is of a more general nature than some of the more popular forms of sport martial arts. Techniques such as punching, kicking, throwing and wrestling are all studied by the student of taijutsu. Once these techniques are learned in the more or less ideal conditions of a dojo, these same techniques are trained under a variety of conditions such as on uneven ground, in water, in the dark and even blindfolded. Added to this type of training is the study of body weak points (and how these same points can be used to promote health and relieve pain), diet, special forms of conditioning and practical psychology. The reason taijutsu covers so many different areas of study is a product of its long history.

Unlike modern martial art forms such as judo, karate or aikido, whose histories are only traceable back one hundred years or so, taijutsu has a history that stretches back centuries. Because of this, the overall aim of taijutsu training (and ninjutsu training on the whole) is different from that of sport forms. This is not to disparage modern forms, as in fact, most long-time practitioners of ninjutsu have at one time or another engaged in either the Japanese sports of kendo, judo or karate, or they have practiced the Western sports of fencing, boxing or wrestling (freestyle and Greco-Roman). These sports, by their very nature, are valuable supplements to taijutsu training. However, anyone training in ninjutsu will always take taijutsu as a foundation to his training.

The insistence on real fighting conditions is one very important reason why taijutsu is so different from other martial art forms. The ninja trainee is expected to be able to perform self-defense techniques regardless of the surface upon which he is standing or the type of clothes he is wearing. While many martial arts allow for competition under set and rigid rules, the ninja begins with the assumption that there are absolutely no rules and "anything goes." Because of this type of thinking, the planning out of strategies, as it is often used in fencing or judo, is simply not possible. Since there is no time for such planning in real self-defense situations, the development of intuition is very important. The wide variety of fighting skills mentioned earlier helps in this training of intuition. So, even though such well-known techniques as roundhouse kicks, side kicks and backfist strikes are not used by the ninja, they must be familiar to be dealt with.

In almost all the classical martial arts of Japan, the concept of "no mind" is used. This idea is called many things such as "mushin," "muso" or "munen muso." It is not the author's intention to try to distinguish all the various meanings these words can have. However, regardless of how one labels this con-

2

cept, it is central to all forms of martial arts as they are practiced in their classical form. Training in a wide variety of techniques is an aid to achieving this state of "no mind."

Like so many other things in life, the achievement of "no mind" has to be experienced to be understood. Fortunately, it is possible to see if a martial artist has reached this stage of development. With "no mind," as in anything else that is naturally human, there are different levels of achievement and understanding. This has nothing to do with a person's rank, school or even the number of students he teaches. In fact, in the author's experience, often the instructors with the greatest number of students do not have the ability to demonstrate or assist a student to achieve "no mind." As mentioned earlier, there are some guidelines when looking at someone's technique that will show the presence of mushin.

First of all, these guidelines apply only when one is watching someone respond to an attack that is not preset. Anyone can look good when he knows exactly what his attacker will do. Granted, even here there is a large difference in people's technique. But in every case where one knows what the attacker will do, the process of having to respond to an uncertain situation is removed. This is one reason it is possible for less than competent men to run fairly successful schools, while in reality, they are not actually teaching anything of substance.

A good indication of an instructor's ability is his talent for keeping long-term students. Too often, instructors keep their students in line by direct intimidation, and as a result lose many students the minute those very same students achieve black belt level. If, on the other hand, someone's technique comes from "no mind," then he rarely has to bother with such games.

Another indication of this state of mind is the speed with which one performs his techniques. If someone appears to be moving in almost slow motion when responding to an unexpected technique then this is a good indication. Of course, he must be successful with his counter, but there is more to this than simply moving slow. To the attacker whose technique was countered, the man who moves from "no mind" will appear to be little more than a blur if he sees him move at all. This somewhat strange situation of slow motion to an outside witness and very fast to an inside witness (the person receiving the technique) is but one of the indications of real martial arts achievement.

Another important characteristic is total lack of hesitation.

Someone whose technique comes from "mushin" (literally, from nothing) does not decide what to do and then do it. Rather, in a very real sense, he does not know what he is going to do until he has already done it.

Lastly, there should be no exaggeration when doing a technique. This is one of the biggest differences between sports martial arts and classical martial arts.

Sportsmen generally end their careers as the benefits of youth begin to fade. Followers of the older ideas of martial arts generally become better with age. Herein lies the key to understanding the aim of taijutsu training.

The aim of taijutsu training, and ninjutsu training as a whole, reflects the long history of the art in that it is not for a specialist. Historically, "ryu" (martial art schools) were places of overall learning. Not only was fighting taught in all its various forms, but also such subjects as strategy, nature observation, medical practices and the fine arts were learned inside these training doors. This type of education helped the trainee to better fit in the society of his day. Contrary to popular belief (generally created by moviemakers who simply are ignorant when it comes to ninjutsu), the historical ninja were rarely found sneaking over castle walls. However, they were often found performing their roles as information gatherers with a sense of social responsibility to their family clans. This same social responsibility, and how one should act while being responsible, were all part of the education gained through the old ryu system.

Basic Basics

Someone once described the things in life that one could not live without as the basic basics. Such things as food, water and shelter are obvious. For the serious martial artist, this expression has a slightly different, but just as important, meaning. It is strange that so many people will invest their time and money in dojo training and then leave their training at their dojo when they go home. The basic basics refer to the training that takes place every day of someone's life and have a much greater influence on one's abilities than most people realize. Unless this training is studied very hard, any martial artist can expect his abilities to start fading as soon as his youth is past.

Probably the most important area of training that is overlooked is diet. It may seem strange to call diet an area of training, but one look at any gathering of people will reveal a substantial group of overweight individuals. It is also not at all uncommon to see so-called martial arts instructors who are obviously overweight. There are, of course, many excuses for this sort of thing, but the only reason anyone becomes overweight is that he simply eats more food than his body needs. Sure, many people like to resort to various excuses about chemical imbalances of the body, and there might even be some grounds to this argument for some people. However, if you take a close look at pictures of people who have spent time in concentration camps, you would be hard pressed to find one overweight person. This is not to belittle the tragedy of such places, but tragedy can be a harsh teacher. The lesson here is clear — anyone can control his weight if he practices discipline.

Once one has his body weight at a good level, then he should still follow a diet that supplies him energy without resulting in the after-meal slump that is so common with today's fast foods. Unquestionably, one of the main problems with diet in America today is the overeating of meats, sugar and overprocessed foods. Individual study of this subject is a must for any serious martial artist (or anyone else for that matter) because diet has a direct bearing on one's energy level and that, in turn, influences one's total being. As general guidelines, the following foods are almost always better than the above mentioned. Fish instead of beef or pork, raw or steamed vegetables instead of overcooked or canned, and fruit instead of donuts, candy, etc. Of course, there is nothing earth-shaking about all this. But as always, knowing something and actually using that knowledge are often two entirely different things.

The next of the basic basics for any martial artist is conditioning. The amount of time wasted in martial arts schools conditioning students is almost unbelievable. Such training as push-ups, sit-ups and other types of basic conditioning should be done at home. To expect a martial arts instructor to "get you in shape" is more or less an insult. If one has to spend all his time with his instructor getting in shape then when does he expect to actually do any real training?

Of all the basic conditioning one has to do, endurance training is by far the most important. (It should be noted that the author did not write aerobics because that is not what he meant. Aerobics are a necessary part of anyone's training, but one should not confuse the fairly simple idea of running or walking around to train one's heart with the much larger idea of endurance). Endurance must be trained mentally. This type of training takes many forms. In the beginning of training, the student often has to perform countless repetitions of the most basic motions. This is necessary for form development, but on a deeper level, it trains the student in patience. Contrary to what seems to be a fashionable belief, ninjutsu is not a shortcut to martial arts mastery. In fact, if anything, the actual techniques are very difficult to learn, and mastery cannot be achieved without years of serious training and study. The purpose of starting the beginning student off with repetitive training is to help him develop the proper mental conditioning so that he can face the long road to skill. This is the type of conditioning the author means when speaking of endurance.

The ability to keep training and studying day after day, month after month and year after year is far more important than being born with talent or having a great teacher. Too many times, the natural athlete will burn out at an early age. While on the other hand, having a great teacher can often lead a student to rely too much on his teacher's directions and opinions, which slows the development of self-confidence and self-reliance. If one develops the patience to keep up his own training, then one's physical training should take care of itself. However, some suggestions can be made as to the nature of basic physical training.

In the author's opinion, probably the most overlooked area of physical training is that of stretching. While it is true that most martial artists stretch before training, they rarely do stretch training for its own sake. This is not good; when one stretches only before training, then the actual training will undo much of the flexibility gained. This is why people are sometimes sore the day following a strenuous workout. In ninjutsu, one is taught to stretch every day for fifteen-to-twenty minutes, or longer if possible. Generally, one does this at night because it can help one relax before sleeping. Also, the body is stiffer in the morning, and consequently, such training as walking, running, swimming or meditation should be done then.

It should be added that all stretching should be done in a slow, relaxed manner. Ballistic or bounce stretching often does more harm than good and can often lead to injury. For taijutsu, stretching should be done to develop flexibility in the inside of the legs to make the rather low and wide stances used possible. Of course, the other joints of the body should be conditioned, but the legs (particularly the inside of the joints) and the back should receive the most attention. It should be noted that if one is studying martial arts as a method of self-defense, then one would be well-advised to remember he will not have time to "loosen up" before defending himself and should train accordingly.

Before leaving the area of conditioning, I would like to make a case for walking over running. The benefits of the "world's oldest exercise" are often overlooked. While it is true running gives a higher return in terms of the amount of stress it places on the body, it also leads to a much higher chance of injury. Generally, these injuries occur in the knees and ankles, and these are the very joints one should keep healthy. Running also has the side effect of shortening the muscles of the legs, which is also just the opposite of what one wants for taijutsu. Of course, it is possible to injure yourself while walking, but such accidents are rare. Walking can also be very relaxing, especially when done in natural settings. Lastly, walking is very similar to the basic footwork used in taijutsu, so when one is out walking, he is in a very real sense training his footwork.

Training Theory

Today, the veil of secrecy surrounding ninjutsu has been lifted. Books abound on such subjects as ninjutsu history, philosophy and weapons. Little, however, has been written about the actual training methods of the ninja. There has been some writing done on the conditioning exercises used, but there is a great difference in the type of training needed to build strength and endurance and the type of training that allows one to face danger with a cool and detached attitude. In this respect, the "how to" of ninja training needs to be addressed. Contrary to popular belief, there are no secret formulas behind the ninja's impressive abilities. Indeed, the only secrets are training skillfully and taking a proper overall approach to the martial arts. Learning proper technique is important, but the ability to actually apply techniques is critical. The following training methods will teach you how to apply techniques under high-stress conditions.

The essence of ninjutsu or ninpo training is the elimination of one's weak points ("suki"). Weak points can take on many forms, from basic physical techniques to the more difficult area of wrong mental outlook. Weak points are thus infinite in their variety, but on the level of physical technique, two stand out in particular: Stance ("kamae") weak points, and its close cousin, tension, are by far the most common errors.

Almost anyone who has been around the martial arts has seen experienced practitioners, who through bad habits or bad training methods, use incorrect or overly tense stances. Often, experienced martial artists get away with this weakness because they have superior strength or speed. This sort of approach works fine — as long as one is confronted by opponents who play speed and strength "contests." The opponent who uses timing and distance control, however, will easily overcome speed and strength.

Stance training is not just standing still in one place in one particular pose. It is also basic footwork. Ideally, one should be able to change direction during any movement (this ability also applies to simply standing in one place in a stance). There are a variety of ways to develop this skill; three will be explained here.

Probably the best form of stance training is walking, running, jumping or technique training on ice. Frozen lakes or iced-over paths are ideal for this. The key is the discovery and control of one's equilibrium while moving. The amount of time even experienced martial artists spend off balance is amazing. However, since almost all their opponents spend just as much time off balance, this situation is generally not noticed. Note that stance training on ice can be used in a variety of places, and depending on one's level of training, it can be combined with some very good forms of mental training.

While living in Germany, the author spent a great deal of time training on the ice and snow covered slopes of the Alps. On one level, this type of training helps one become fairly indifferent to the cold. But on a much more important level, training under conditions where the slightest slip can have rather serious consequences, such as quickly becoming a rather colorful part of the landscape, forces the trainee to totally focus on the present moment. Present moment awareness is very important in taijutsu.

If ice is unavailable, then wet grass or tile surfaces can be used. It is also possible to polish a floor and then cover it with light powder before training. As mentioned earlier, this training develops a high awareness of balance, and this in turn, makes it possible to throw an opponent with a minimum of motion. Once one always stands in balance, one can sense any little break in the opponent's balance.

The other common weak area is excessive tension. Many martial artists believe they can use tension and breathing techniques to stop an opponent's punch or kick from hurting. Unfortunately, there are plenty of points on the body that can be neither tensed nor reinforced through muscle development. This is why, in ninjutsu, the practitioner must train to be totally relaxed no matter what is happening to him.

Once Dr. Hatsumi was asked how one could possibly escape a perfect joint lock. His reply was to let the opponent break your arm, then counterattack when he showed a weak point.

This may sound radical, and it brought little comfort to those who were expecting some secret to let them escape unhurt. However, escaping totally unscathed is not always possible. Thus, the ability to perform a few techniques (or even one technique) with this attitude of staying relaxed and flexible — regardless of what the opponent does — is far more important than having a collection of techniques that only work in ideal situations.

The key to eliminating weak points is discovering how not to lose. Since there will always be stronger or faster opponents, common sense dictates finding a method by which one can overcome any seeming disadvantage. As one eliminates one's weak points, one discovers that it is quite impossible to force victory. Making the first move and defeating an opponent is only possible when he has a real weak point. His weak point can be on either the physical or mental level, but one or both must be present before you attack.

Interestingly, the so-called positive schools of Japanese kenjutsu ("sword technique") that were noted for their highly aggressive attacking style did not really violate this weak point principle. In effect, these schools used their attacking style to "draw out" a weak-point from the opponent. The key to performing this type of attack is distance. The fakes used by these schools are almost always done out of range. Thus, when the opponent tries to counter the fake, he actually sets himself within striking distance. In effect, he steps right into the attacker's technique.

There is another approach that uses attacking to draw out a weak point. It is based on rhythm. This approach was made famous by the well-known Musashi. However, here to, the opponent has to be drawn into his own defeat. In either case, if the opponent shows no weak point, then any attack against him will necessarily open the attacker's own weak points, and the attacker will lose.

To better understand taijutsu, one must examine the different levels of training. First, one must understand that the majority of training in almost all martial arts is not "shin ken gata" or "real fighting technique." Two-man forms, sparring, bag work, road work and most forms of sensitivity training are merely just preparation for training in shin ken gata. In taijutsu, all these preliminary exercises are called "kata geiko," which means "training forms" or "techniques study."

Kata geiko training is varied, but the thing that distinguishes this type of training is its predictability and lack of real danger. Even in such sports as kendo or karate, one is in reality only doing kata geiko when sparring because the opponent's ability to inflict damage is limited. In kendo, one is covered with body armor and the "shinai" (bamboo sword) is fairly innocuous when compared with a sword. In most forms of empty-hand sparring, body targets are limited, and often, the hands are padded. It should also be added that in both kendo and karate, wrestling is generally not allowed. This is not to say that such training is unnecessary; nothing could be further from the truth. Without kata geiko training, one cannot possibly develop the skills needed for the study of shin ken gata.

The majority of training done in bujinkan ninjutsu dojos falls into the category of kata geiko. The reason is fairly simple: Kata geiko is concerned with physical skills training; shin ken gata is the mental training that makes it possible for the martial artist to apply kata geiko.

The many stories of trained fighting experts losing to less experienced opponents can be accounted for by saying that the expert's training lacked an understanding of shin ken gata. Thus, a fairly unskilled opponent, who is actually "uneducated" to the real dangers of fighting, can often overcome a trained fighter because the trained fighter's very training actually gets in his way. That is, because the trained fighter has been educated, his reactions are often inhibited by his desire to select a specific technique, or more likely, he is just plain scared because he has a good understanding of how dangerous real fighting is.

There is absolutely nothing wrong with fear. In its purest form, fear is just energy, like any other emotion. It is only when this energy combines itself with self-awareness and imagination that a trained fighter will freeze-up or over-react. This type of reaction must be overcome through shin ken gata training.

A good example of how this fear reaction works can be seen in the following experiment: An instructor should take a padded stick and stand about six feet from a student. He should tell the student what type of blow to expect, and the student should wait to the last instant before avoiding the attack; grabbing or blocking the stick is not allowed. The student should avoid the strike by using proper footwork. The instructor should check the student's timing and level of overall body tenseness.

Next, the instructor should speed up the attack until he is attacking full-speed. Generally, as the attacks speed up, the student's timing becomes less accurate because of the speed of the attack. Also, his motions will become much larger than needed.

This process should be repeated with a "bokken" (wooden sword), a dull metal sword and a real, sharpened blade. Since that student always knows what attack to expect, this exercise only approaches shin ken gata when done with the real sword. However, this too is very limited. While it is true that real swords are very dangerous, if the attack is limited to only one type of attack then it is very easy to avoid.

This type of training can be continued with padded sticks or bokken so that different attacks are introduced, until the student has to react to whatever the instructor does. For example, after the student can react properly to a straight downward cut ("me uchi"), then he should learn to react to angled downward cuts or sideward cuts ("do uchi"). This gives five possible attacks. Next, a straight thrust ("tsuki") is added; this can be followed by odd-angled cuts to the legs as well as cuts that travel from a low to high line. Timing in these drills is critical. The trainee must move at the last possible instant, or he will be taken in by every fake.

Why train like this with a sword? First of all, a sword moves faster than the hand or foot. Also, one has more angles of attack when wielding a sword. There is also a big reach disadvantage the defender must overcome if he wishes to take the opponent's sword. Lastly, and most important, a sword is generally a "no touch" weapon; while sticks can be caught, it is generally inadvisable to catch a sword by its blade.

The reason for this long process of moving up to training with real weapons is not always obvious. However, it is not possible to submit to such training without acquiring some degree of mastery over timing.

Mastering of timing is very important for any martial art. Any technique done with close to perfect timing simply cannot be countered. This is one reason why experienced martial artists who are actually somewhat out of shape can easily overcome less experienced but much stronger and better conditioned opponents. Whereas one's conditioning changes constantly, one's level of achievement with timing is more or less permanent. Thus, if one can walk, then he can use timing to naturally overcome his opponent.

It should be added that if one uses exact timing, he will not be fooled by fakes or tricks. In his famous book, "Go Rin No Sho," Musashi states that the basis of his system is timing and rhythm. In the very same vein, timing is given a central position of study in taijutsu. It should be added that, in the author's experience, most martial artists move too much, too soon and then, too fast. If one's timing is exact, then speed per se is not necessary. Well-timed motions will blend with those of the opponent in terms of speed and power.

Tactics and Intuition

Along with the study of techniques as a method of developing the proper mental state, the study of overall tactics is also very important. In fact, the usage of tactical tricks has more than once saved someone when he was confronted by an opponent who was technically stronger.

The proper use of tactics is rarely written about because almost every tactical guideline has its exceptions. In this chapter, the author will attempt to explain basic combat tactics as they apply to the study of classical martial arts. The guidelines given can be applied to both armed and unarmed technique. However, since the author wishes to give the reader a sense for what goes into the development of intuition, these ideas are expressed along with the other ideas that apply to taijutsu.

The author acknowledges that a thoughtful reader should be able to formulate very good arguments to contradict much of what is written here. However, while such arguments are very useful in learning, and while there may be several sides to every story, one must begin somewhere.

One of the oldest combat tactics is the proper use of light. Regardless of the source, one should endeavor to have the brightest light behind him. To do this, one should place himself between the light source and the opponent. Not only does this tactic work well for martial artists on the ground, but the old World War I saying, "A Hun in the Sun," shows just how well German pilots understood this idea too! In old Japan, the famous Miyamoto Musashi was notorious for arriving late for duels. While this habit was undoubtedly irksome to Musashi's opponents, it was far from an idiosyncrasy on his part. Since duels were fought at given times, whoever showed up last could approach his opponent with the sun to his back. Also, by showing up late, Musashi could wait until the sun was high enough (at morning) or low enough (at evening) so that it would be just above the horizon. Thus, when Musashi's opponent squared off, he found himself looking directly into the sun. Needless to say, many of Musashi's opponents (many would say victims) never saw what hit them.

Another tactic related to the proper use of light is that of carrying a flashlight at night. When confronting an opponent, the light is shined into his eyes and then quickly shut off. This will temporarily blind the opponent. Of course, if the flashlight is heavy, it can be used as a club or throwing weight once the opponent is blinded. Interestingly, the sword masters of Napoleonic France developed the use of the directional lantern and sword to such a high degree that it was made a criminal offense (with harsh punishments) to be caught carrying both items at night. To understand just how powerful this tactic is, one should take a common flashlight outside at night and conduct his own experiments.

A different set of tactics has to do with the use of the ground and obstacles. "Choose the higher ground" is a maxim as old as military technique. While it is true that ducking and moving in under an opponent's technique can be effective, it is difficult to do this if one has to move uphill to the opponent. Being higher is preferred because blows directed downward are more powerful than those directed upward. Also, when in groups, the higher group can easily hide their numbers whereas the lower group cannot.

Of course, if one finds himself lower than the opponent, all is not lost. However, the lower-standing person should stick to more compact stances and not be over eager to attack. The higher or uphill person can use more open stances and bolder motions because just standing higher than his opponent gives him a reach advantage, and at the same time, moves his head and chest (two prime targets) away from the opponent. While what is written here about the advantages of the higher ground is intended for martial artists, the author would like to note that the United States' recent decision to construct a space-born defensive system (SDI) is in reality nothing more than an extreme application of the "higher ground" principle (No small wonder the other side is more than a little concerned about the whole thing).

Obstacles can also be used to one's advantage. In a natural setting, trees and large rocks can be used to shield one from the opponent. In the city, trash cans, telephone booths or lamp posts can also be used. Not only can obstacles be used as shields, but opponents can always be thrown, pushed or backed into solid objects. Small objects such as sticks, rocks, trash can lids, etc., can also be used to trip up an unwary opponent. Also, such objects can be thrown.

Distracting the opponent, either through physical means or psychological misdirection, is also very important. Physical distractions can be anything from simply throwing a handful of dirt into the opponent's face to more esoteric weapons such as shuriken or spray chemicals.

The main principle is to hit the opponent while staying outside the reach of his weapon. The reason the author calls this tactic distraction is that these type of weapons are not really intended to kill or maim the opponent. These weapons are used to help in escaping. Also along these lines are throwing obstacles in the way of a pursuer. Caltrops or shuriken, thrown directly into the ground so that one point sticks straight up, are good methods to slow down a pursuer.

Psychological misdirection is an endless area of study. Whole martial art systems have grown up around just this one aspect. From Japan, no other art takes more advantage of psychological misdirection than ninjutsu. From China, the art of monkey style kung-fu is influenced by the idea of making the opponent overconfident. Even the famed fencing schools of Renaissance Italy often used misdirection to finish off an opponent before he knew what hit him. Since the warriors of so many cultures resorted to misdirection, it is logical to say that if one's martial art does not take this into account, then one is deluding himself. Instruction that trains one to deal with misdirection must do much more than teach one how to tell the difference between a fake and a real attack.

One of the reasons older martial artists can defeat younger and stronger opponents is that experience has shown them how to use misdirection so that younger opponents defeat themselves. (It should be added that more experienced martial artists usually have a more highly developed intuition; but as always, seeing is believing, and such claims should be examined in the light of common sense). Misdirection is not just the use of fakes and fancy techniques, but more a process of making the opponent believe in something that is not present in the situation. A skilled fighter may put on an act of being scared or drunk to make the opponent overconfident. Faking an injury from a less-than-exact blow would work very much in the same way. It should be noted that every one of these tricks has as its goal the "stopping" of the opponent's mind. That is, his mind will for a very short instant focus on the unexpected actions of his opponent, and this "mental stopping" is what causes his defeat. On a larger scale, this same type of idea was used by armies when they placed dummy cannons on the walls of their castles to make the opposing army believe it was facing a better-armed opponent. The point in learning how to protect oneself against these tricks is to realize the meaning of "zanshin" through training.

Zanshin has been translated into many different forms; but almost all of them lose some part of this concept's true meaning. For the sake of one's personal training, however, the author would advise the reader not to think of zanshin just in terms of the martial arts. Zanshin is the natural outgrowth of long and intensive training and will reflect in a person's everyday actions. A person thus accomplished will show a direct grasp of situations and be able to act quickly and decisively without the usual doubts that trouble the average, untrained person. There will also be a sense of appropriateness in what he does, but it will not always be obvious at first glance. It should be noted here that, according to classical martial arts philosophy, there is no real difference in a person' mental state and his actions. If a person has achieved a certain level of skill, then his technique will reflect that realization. Rank, school, where someone trained, and who trained him is, in the final analysis, irrelevant since his achievement should speak for itself without needing a political backup.

Of course, no discussion of tactics would be complete without the subject of surprise. In fact, it would be fair to say that much of what is known as tactics is really nothing more than the scientific application of surprise. Unquestionably, the best way to attack or counterattack someone is by doing or making something happen that is totally outside his realm of expectation.

A good example would be dropping to the ground and begging for mercy, then attacking the opponent when his guard slackens. Making the unexpected happen is not as clear but just as effective. An example of this would be knocking an obstacle over so that it falls on the opponent, or quickly killing whatever light source is available. The point is to take advantage of the opponent's lack of attention. This is critical, because even if one masters technique and tactics, it is still impossible to force victory on any given opponent unless that opponent participates to some extent in his own defeat. Of course, not being properly trained is just one form of participation.

As mentioned earlier, tactics are an almost unlimited area of study. However, a couple of simple awareness games can help:

First, go into any average room and look around to see what common, everyday items would make good throwing weapons. At first, the list would seem endless, but many objects are wired or plugged into the wall — also, some are too lightweight to do any damage. Next, pick out the items that would make good shields with which to hold off an opponent. For example, a chair is good for shielding oneself from a knife attack. But then, that same chair is fairly useless against a gun unless one can manage to club the attacker before he gets his weapon out.

This type of realization is important, because some tactics work well against some attacks and not at all against others. Just because one is faced with a gun-bearing opponent does not mean all is lost (although things are generally a little more difficult). Generally, however, if one's attacker intends to shoot him straight away, then he will probably never see the gun anyway. The same could be said about any other weapon. By developing one's sixth sense, hopefully one will help his chances of escaping.

On the subject of guns, two interesting quotes can be given. First, the founder of aikido, Uyeshiba Morihei, once said, "It is a long time between a man's decision to shoot you and his action of pulling the trigger." Second, when asked what he would do if faced with a gunman who was out of reach, ninjutsu Grandmaster Dr. Masaaki Hatsumi said simply, "Ask for Divine guidance." To the author these two answers say the same thing and should be pondered deeply.

Another method that can be used to learn a sense for tactics is playing an adult form of hide and seek. The current game played with paint pistols is one example. However, it is important to realize the shortcomings of this type of game. While it is true that one's awareness can be refined, the weapons used in real life have a longer range — meaning that this type of game can be useful for short-range self-defense but is fairly useless for many forms of military activity.

Tactics, their applications, and the ways of training to use them are almost endless. Being aware of your surroundings and what elements can be used to your advantage are two very important aspects of successful combat tactics. Expertise in weaponry and unarmed defense can prove inadequate if you don't become equally expert in the psychology of combat and the utilization of everything at one's disposal.

Martial Arts Attention

Anyone who has ever tried to teach a child knows just how important proper attention is. In the case of a beginning martial artist, wandering attention is often just as big an obstacle as physical conditioning. While it is true that consistent attention can be developed in a fairly new student, the training of attention for more advanced practitioners is often overlooked. Why? Because the type and quality of attention an instructor-level martial artist needs is radically different from that of a beginner.

In the beginning, a student must learn to totally focus on the words and actions of his teacher and training partner. In addition to regular training, the student is often taught simple mental techniques such as concentrating on his breathing, following his thoughts or basic visualizations. The importance of this type of training is in its ability to stabilize one's mental/emotional processes. Oddly enough, many instructors feel that once they have developed a fairly stable character, they "have arrived." This is understandable. Once one develops some degree of control over his attention, a great increase in confidence is only natural. However, in the martial arts, as with everything else that lives according to the laws of nature, there is no "have arrived," only "arriving."

Thus, in reality, once one has developed a fairly stable attention, then (and only then) can one begin approaching the real study of attention.

Unlike the stable, well-focused attention mentioned earlier, an advanced martial artist must work so that his attention is diffused a full 360 degrees around him. This is necessary because of the weak points caused by concentrating on one opponent or even in one direction. Unlike sporting contests that are fought in the arena, real life attacks can and usually do come from either the side or back. This is only natural because anyone attempting a surprise attack would attack in such a manner so as to ensure the success of the attack. The development of martial arts such as "iaijutsu," and later, "iaido" (the technique of drawing a sword) reflect their creator's awareness of this basic principle of attack. Thus, in the case of iaido one learns to draw his sword and cut in response to attacks from behind, the side, and of course, the front. In the same sense, one should learn to respond to attacks with this unarmed technique regardless of the attack's angle. This can require a lot of study because most martial arts, as they are practiced today, only consider an attack from the front. This is often made worse by limiting the allowable targets. Thus in kendo, one is allowed to strike only the head, body (stomach), hands and throat. Strikes to the legs are not allowed. While this type of thinking makes for a very enjoyable sporting contest, these types of rules were never observed by either the samurai or ninja.

While training in the Kashima style of sword fencing, the author was exposed to an entire range of techniques that attacked the legs with the sword. Generally, one is told that such techniques will not work because of the sword's length. However, as the author learned to his surprise (and occasional chagrin), these techniques work very well indeed. It should be added that those particular techniques belong to the school's "Okuden" (secret techniques), but getting oneself killed by a secret technique is, in the final analysis, no more pleasant than being struck down with the most basic technique. The lesson here is clear: Whether learning to deal with the rather restricted field of frontal attacks or the somewhat more difficult field of general attacks, one is simply not allowed to make assumptions of any kind. Of course, in the beginning of training, the simplest way to learn techniques is with the opponent facing you. But this is really only part of the beginning stage of attention development. The point of all this is that one must construct drills and training practices that will expand his attention.

Knowing a Martial Arts Style

Regardless of the style or philosophy used by a martial artist, his motions and his overall approach will be greatly influenced by the particular school in which he has been trained. That is, to a great extent, each person has a base from which he learns about other arts. To cite two very well-known examples: Aikido, which was the creation of Morihei Uyeshiba, uses a type of body motion that reflects Uyeshiba's extensive training in kenjutsu and aikijutsu. Thus in aikido, one will find a great deal more footwork than in most other modern practices. In the case of jeet kune do, which was the creation of Bruce Lee, Lee's training in wing chun kung-fu is very evident. Once again, the actual techniques may have been somewhat altered, but the real basics (in terms of footwork, timing and rhythm) do not differ significantly from the system's founder's early training. This understanding is very important when anyone tries to move from one martial art to another. Someone switching from an attack-oriented system such as boxing (Western style or Eastern styles such as wing chun or Thai boxing) can have some very real difficulties when moving to a more defensive based martial art such as aikido or taijutsu. By the same token, the reverse is also true when moving from defensive to offensive systems. Some day in the distant future this problem may not exist as more and more martial artists become skilled in a number of culturally different arts. However, in the meantime, some observations on the general structures of martial arts may help the reader understand how and why certain martial arts developed the way they did. This will, in turn, help the reader understand not only the art of taijutsu but, hopefully, his own.

Whenever one looks at any martial art he almost immediately asks where the system originated. He will be told in what country, who founded the art, and when. That is usually as far as the conversation goes.

This is really sad because these surface answers almost always contain the information needed to understand any martial art if people would just stop and examine the information. Surprisingly, the keys to understanding any martial art are almost always overlooked as soon as the idly curious have had a couple of questions answered. With a little digging, one can uncover a great deal of information and understanding on just about any martial art. As an example, let's look at the martial arts of Japan.

To anyone experienced with military history, the Japanese martial arts are strangely lacking in a couple of very important techniques. The first of these is the total lack of the use of handheld shields. The other is even stranger for a culture that has had countless men devote their lives to the study of sword technique. This, of course, is Japan's almost total lack of a fencing technique known as the lunge.

In the case of shields, the author has heard a number of very interesting explanations. Some are fairly good, and some are outright ridiculous. Probably the silliest idea is that such shields would not stop (or for the true believer, not even slow down) a Japanese sword. While it may be true that the Japanese sword is very sharp, it is doubtful that their edges were any sharper than swords made in other parts of the world (ex. Damascus). It is, of course, true that if a shield is struck at the exact proper angle on its edge, the sword can cut through part of it. But it should be added that this is a double-edged situation because, more often than not, the sword becomes lodged in the shield, leaving the attacking swordsman in a less-than-enviable position. So any arguments centered around the cutting power of the Japanese sword as a reason for the lack of Japanese shields can be discarded.

Perhaps a better place to look would be the actual type of fighting done by the Japanese during the pre-Edo period. During this period, the sword was, in all probability, not even a major battlefield weapon. The bow and arrow, the spear, and its cousin, the naginata, were the weapons of choice. Why? Well for a number of very good reasons. First of all, the spear and naginata are far easier to use than swords. Also, these two weapons are much more effective against cavalry than any but the largest swords because of their reach advantage. Lastly, the halberd and the bow and arrow usually develop earlier in a culture's history than the sword. These points are of interest because of their bearing on the question of the Japanese shield. All of these weapons (spear, naginata and bow) require the use of both hands. What body protection that was used took the form of armor. At the time in question, before A.D 1600, the Japanese did not use a shield because they simply did not have a free arm on which to hang it. After the period of Warring States, the shield was not carried simply because no one thought about it. Japan was isolated, and martial arts were actually fairly restricted when compared with the number and type of weapons used in Europe 1600-1900. This restriction from the outside world is one reason the classical martial arts of Japan, such as ninjutsu, are so valuable as a link to the past.

The case for the Japanese not having a lunge is also interesting and no less important if one wishes to really grasp both the strong and weak points of that country's martial arts. Unquestionably, the lunge is one of the most deadly moves used in any form of sword play. And yet, much of the move's danger is removed if one is familiar and practiced at countering it. But, for the unwary, the lunge will often hit before they have seen their opponent move. There are many historical accounts of Italian fencers (the Italians developed the lunge in the 1500s) striking down opponents before anyone had seen what had happened. Many authorities have pointed out that the Japanese sword was designed to be used with two hands, which more or less rules out the lunge. This is simply not so. The author has found a number of references to the use of the lunge with a two-handed sword in books written A.D. 1500-1600 in Europe.

Another interesting but useless argument centers around the idea that the further East one goes from Europe, the less one sees the use of the point in fencing; cutting becomes the only form of attack used. Once again, this sounds good but does not hold water when examined in the light of historical research. There is one reason why the Japanese did not develop the lunge, and it has nothing to do with the swords they used or where they are located on that West-to-East cutting map. In the author's opinion, the reason the Japanese never developed the lunge can be found in their diet. I don't mean their diet today, I mean their diet before the modern age. According to accounts written by European visitors to Japan during the period around 1600, the Japanese had a physical build very different from that of the Europeans. Unlike Europeans, who were actually fairly tall, the Japanese at that time, and even today, were on the average quite short. Combined with this was a set of body proportions that were also very different. According to accounts written at that time, the Japanese had long torsos and short legs. If this is true, and there is no reason to believe that it is not, then it is totally logical that there is no Japanese lunge. Since a man's reach with a lunge is determined by his legs and not his arms, anyone built with short legs would find this move useless.

Of course, the body type of any group of people is influenced by genetics, but diet is particularly important during childhood. Since World War II, the Japanese have altered their diet to include a wider variety of foods. This, according to some authorities, has led to a very real shift in their overall height and general build.

The above examples are just two points that really need to be addressed if one wishes to grasp a broad understanding of ninjutsu or any other martial art. It should be added that ninjutsu is very different than standard Japanese martial arts. This is not surprising since many of the techniques used by the historical ninja originally came from China. For example, Dr. Hatsumi is the 28th Headmaster of the Gyokko ryu. The Gyokko ryu is named after a Chinese monk named Gyokko who taught the system's founder, Hakunnsai Tozawa. Interestingly, the "kihon happo" (8 basic techniques) of Dr. Hatsumi's style come directly from the Gyokko ryu. Another important influence on ninjutsu, as it exists today, has to be the many years spent in China by Dr. Hatsumi's teacher, Toshitsugu Takamatsu. This influence is hard to define in terms of actual techniques, but Takamatsu's willingness to travel abroad (often in less than safe conditions) is probably one reason why the master teachers of today, Dr. Hatsumi included, have shown such a willingness to travel to other countries rather than to just sit back and be indifferent to what other cultures have to offer. (For the uninformed reader, the Japanese do not usually travel abroad alone, and when they do, they are not always the "ideal tourist." In this respect, the trips made by Japan's many high-level martial artists have done a great deal in helping bridge the huge cultural gap between our two countries).

In terms of actual techniques, taijutsu uses stances that are much lower and wider than most other martial arts. It takes a long time to reach the point where one can actually move with these stances. Of course, one could allow the students to cheat themselves and not take the time to learn their stances properly, but this would cause the student more harm than good in the long run. In this respect, the ninja reflect a somewhat Chinese attitude of teaching and training the students properly in the basics. If one tries to jump to high-level techniques before he has a good grounding in the basics, he will always forget those high-level techniques very quickly. However, if the basics are trained properly, then higher-level techniques will come very naturally. Also, techniques learned in this fashion will not be forgotten because they will have been learned with the body and not just the mind.

When one studies the art of ninjutsu, one will very quickly run into the idea of doing things naturally. (If one's teacher says he is teaching ninjutsu and doesn't bring up the subject, then go find another school because doing things naturally is central to ninjutsu technique and philosophy.) What is meant by doing things naturally is easier to demonstrate than write about, but here again, some ideas can be given. First and foremost, any technique that is done naturally will show a lack of excessive tension. Even when under great pressure, if one is acting naturally, his body will be relaxed and free from excessive tension. In taijutsu, tension usually shows up in the student's shoulders, but too much tension in the hips and arms is not uncommon.

Another indication is the speed with which one does his techniques. While it would be nice to be so fast one could strike an opponent before he knows what it was all about, such speed is, in the final analysis, impossible. (If one is getting hit by someone that seems to move that fast, then the author's advice would be to go back and study basic distance because he is, unquestionably, getting too close to you and attacking the instant you step forward into that "too close" range).

One's speed should always fit to a particular situation. Trying to move fast on broken or wet ground is one sure way to find oneself falling down in a rather graceless way. Also, one's motions should be in harmony with the opponent's. It is true that one can use disrupting rhythm to defeat an opponent, but this is only possible if one understands harmonious motion in the first place. If one's motions are in harmony with the opponent's, then he will move at the speed dictated by the situation and not according to how fast he can go.

Another aspect of natural movement is its lack of rigidity. This can be confusing for the beginner because he is told on one side that the basic techniques have to be learned exactly, and then he is told that there is no real "given" way to do any one technique. Actually, both of these pieces of advice are correct but at very different times in a person's training.

At the beginning of training, one should in fact work very hard to learn the basic forms exactly. This exactness is important because one will not have time to stop and try to remember how to do a technique later. In a very real sense, at this stage one is programming one's body with specific information on how to move according to the principles of his particular martial art. Later, one must train so that his body can take advantage of the programming learned earlier. This training can take on a variety of forms, from free sparring to relfex drills. However, they all have in common the need to react accurately to an attack that is not given in a preset fashion. It should be noted that this type of training has to be very general in nature to really achieve its aim. If one trains in just one restricted area (ex. free sparring), then one could still very easily lose when faced with the unexpected such as an unusual weapon or a less-than-ideal environment.

Before leaving the subject of understanding how to make a general approach to any style, it is important to bring up the area of personal interpretation. Any martial art is subject to the same forces of interpretation as any other human activity. If someone were to watch three different ninjutsu instructors perform the same technique, he probably would not notice a big difference in what was happening. However, if one slowed everything down, then the timing, angling and overall body movements would be very different. This, of course, does not even include the so-called "spiritual" outlook of the three instructors, which is very difficult for the untrained to notice. The point is more or less obvious; the techniques are different because everyone is built slightly differently and has different (sometimes radically) outlooks. In truth, even today, there is not a single, true style of taijutsu, because all the active instructors stress different areas of training. This is not to say that anyone who buys a black suit is a ninja. Rather, if an instructor's abilities prove themselves on a consistent basis, then it is very difficult to be honestly negative about what he is doing. Of course, any instructor should have some type of connection to an acknowledged teacher in whatever style he is teaching. However, here too, there is no guarantee that just because someone has a piece of paper some type of magic power is bestowed upon him. Also a "connection" can take on many forms.

Lastly, the reader is to be warned that people decide they are ready to teach at very different levels of their training. The well-known 16th-century warrior, Musashi, did not feel he was ready to teach until he was over 50 (and that was after he had fought in around 60 duels and a war). On the other hand, there are plenty of instructors with schools who are still in their twenties. In general, the author prefers to associate with older instructors who are well-traveled. Generally, these type of men have enough experience and can help others see how martial arts can be used for something other than simple self-defense or sport. Generally, gray hair (or no hair at all), grandchildren and the ability to speak a few languages (learned in whatever country the language is native to) are all good indications. There are, of course, a few good young instructors, but they have more or less eluded the author.

It should be noted that as of this year, 1986, ninjutsu is still a very young martial art in America, and as of today, the majority of instructors are still fairly young and still have years ahead to continue growing.

The Ninja's Self-Training

It has been said that only about one in every two thousand martial arts students become an instructor. To this, it should probably be added that only about one in every ten thousand instructors becomes a master. There are, of course, many reasons for this. Some authorities would claim that people today will not follow instructors the way they used to. Others would claim that today's life-style is the wrong environment within which to train. Finally, there are those who claim that masters are more myth than fact and that such a level of skill does not really exist. All of these reasons have some claim to truth, but each and every one of them overlooks the critical issue of self-training.

The longer someone is in the martial arts, the more important self-training becomes. While an instructor can maintain his level of skill by teaching classes, real improvement can only come by the lonely process of self-training.

Miyamoto Musashi was an example of what can be done through self-training. Although he received very little formal training, he is remembered today as Japan's greatest swordsman. Practically all of his skill and accomplishments rested on an almost inhuman program of self-training. Today, Musashi's program would be impossible to follow. However, the spirit of his effort can be followed in a more balanced manner.

Before actually beginning self-training, it is important to realize a few things about it. First, persistence and patience are more important than an occasional frantic outburst. As a person collects experience, it takes longer and longer training intervals to show any real improvement. Most experienced martial artists have experienced such "dry spells" and learned that about all one can do is wait it out. Secondly, self-training can sometimes be exasperating. Since one is working to eliminate weak points, this means spending long hours working on the things one has difficulty with. It can also mean working on things one is not interested in. Generally, people are most skilled in areas that interest them. Areas that are boring or overly difficult get ignored. This is exactly the sort of thing that self-training should correct. Lastly, self-training does not "count" in most dojo. Often rank has less to do with a person's skill than the amount of time he is in a dojo. This is, of course, a tradition, and no judgment is passed here. The important point is that all self-training is totally personal. If all this seems to make self-training a rather thankless task, that is because in some respects it is. However, self-training is the only chance a martial artist has of ever reaching a very high level of skill. If there is a positive side to self-training, it is the high level of skill and overall self-mastery it makes possible.

The number of forms self-training takes is almost limitless. However, the ninja have always kept their training close to nature. Here, some of their ideas and methods are given. This particular type of training can be adapted to fit both the city and the country environments, and it does not matter what type of martial art with which a person begins. Just as self-training transcends style, so too these drills are appropriate for any martial artist.

The first set of exercises are designed to develop overall agility and endurance. Whereas heavy bag or speed bag work can help develop hands and feet, the ability to move the entire body quickly and smoothly is often overlooked. Also, since real fighting skills are rarely used in ideal situations (such as in a dojo), such training will help enable the ninja to automatically adapt to any environment.

A simple exercise for developing agility is running in wooded areas. The area should be such that one cannot run more than a few yards before dodging around a tree or under a limb. This type of running should be done as fast as possible. An extension of this training is obstacle course running. These courses can be set up anywhere, from a wooded area to a city alley. Such courses should add climbing, crawling and jumping over things to the obstacles presented by the first drill. Training on such courses is one of the sources of the ninja's ability to escape or simply outrun his usually slower opponents.

Striking a variety of targets is useful for a variety of purposes. To begin with, the trainee should strike the target by just extending the hand or foot that is used. Next, a step should be added, but the arm or leg should not be extended. Lastly comes the full-power blow using the fist or foot with total body motion behind the strike.

Care must be taken to prevent injuries. This is particularly the case with strikes that use the fingertips and toes. It should be noted that the real point of this type of training is not being able to break objects but rather to hit a target with the fist and body aligned for as much power as possible. Too much of this type of training is not good and only leads to permanent injury to the body.

To train for accurate strikes, the following exercise can be used. Take a bottle of common soap bubbles and have a training partner blow bubbles. Use the bubbles for targets. Because the bubbles fly in odd patterns and are made in groups, it is possible to train accurate, multiple strikes. In this exercise, kicks can be combined with punches for better training.

The use of a blindfold will increase overall awareness. There are several ways to approach this training. One method is to take a few hours and wear a blindfold around one's house. It is often surprising what can be learned by such a simple experiment. If training in groups, it is possible to string a thin rope over a fairly simple course and have blindfolded trainees follow the course. Care should be taken so that dangerous situations will not arise. These courses should be followed at a slow but purposeful pace. Of course, training of any type done in the dark is good for developing awareness. Just walking at night in areas (such as the countryside with little light) is good training.

One of the most important elements in any martial arts training is the repetition of basic motions. This is probably the origin of the various kata methods used by most arts. Even such basic motions as walking and running need to be studied deeply. The proper application of the simplest motion, such as a kick or punch, can take years to learn. In taijutsu, long walks are used as one method to train the most basic motion in a variety of conditions. This would seem simple until one tries to walk up the side of an ice-covered mountain or on a frozen lake. If this type of training is done properly, the transition to techniques used on difficult terrain is not only easier but will proceed in a safer fashion.

Although not a part of classical training, the spread of information has made it possible for the modern martial artist to read and study about a variety of styles from various cultures. This study must be followed up by practicing various arts. Thus, such arts as kendo, judo, boxing, wrestling and fencing have a place in training. A wide variety of training will make one's understanding of his own art much deeper. In fact, in today's world, if one is not versed in several martial arts then he is not really a martial artist at all.

It is better if these arts come from a variety of cultures because martial arts vary fundamentally from one culture to the next — based on differences in dress, battle tactics, armor and even the build of the people that evolved the art.

Self-training is an almost unlimited area of study. The ideas given here are some of those used in practicing ninjutsu. The role and importance of self-training should never be overlooked. It is one of the main differences between an instuctor and a master instructor.

Part II

Techniques

The purpose of the following section is to show how the basic movements of taijutsu are related to more difficult techniques. Since martial arts is a limitless study, this section can do little more than serve as an indicator. The reader is encouraged to study on his own and use the information presented here to discover new techniques and applications. Since taijutsu incorporates all the motions of martial arts, such as punching, kicking, throwing, joint locks, etc., it would be impossible to do more than give some basic (but very important) techniques and show how these same techniques can be used in a variety of situations. It is hoped by the author that this approach will give the reader a feeling for taijutsu.

It should be noted that the principles outlined in the author's book, "Traditional Ninja Weapons," would also apply to the techniques in these sections. In the final analysis, the basic motions do not change, yet each weapon has its own principles of use. It should also be noted that unarmed technique is considered to be more important than armed technique. However, if one is not familiar with weapon principles, then unarmed defense against weapons is somewhat difficult.

Basic Stances

There are a variety of stances used in taijutsu. In the beginning of training, stances are used as models from which techniques are performed. Later, the concept of stance should become so much a part of a martial artist that he does not need the concept of stance. It is important when standing in a stance that one be able to move in any direction with freedom of movement so as not to telegraph what one will do.

The stances in taijutsu usually take the form of an L or T stance; this means the front foot is pointed directly at the opponent while the back foot is at a 90-degree angle to the front foot. The level (height) of the stance will always depend on the circumstance. For example, it is generally not a good idea to use very low stances on wet or uneven ground. However, if one is unarmed and facing a weapon, then a low stance will present the opponent with a smaller target.

Common stances in taijutsu are fudo no kamae (1), hoe no kamae (2), doko no kamae front & side view (3 & 4), ichimonji no kamae front & side view (5 & 6), jumonji no kamae front & side view (7 & 8), hicho no kamae front & side view (9 & 10) and kosa no kamae front & side view (11 & 12).

Some common mistakes in stances can be seen in the following examples: Front foot should be pointed straight ahead, not inward (1). Front knee should be pointing straight ahead, not turned inward (2). Front foot should point forward, and the back foot should be flat on the ground (3). Hands should be held relaxed in front of the body, not pulled in (4). There is too much tension in

the upper back, and the back hand should be more forward in a natural position (5). Hands and elbows are too high, this indicates excess tension in the upper body (6). Front leg is too straight to allow freedom of movement (7). Hands are held too high, once again indicating excess tension (8).

Basic Motion

The most basic motion of taijutsu is sunshi no kata. This motion is done in a very relaxed manner, there is no snap at the end of the motion. The attitude is one of not having a particular will to hit or fight. This attitude is basic to taijutsu when doing techniques.

From a natural starting pose (1) the motion is done by stepping forward (2)

and letting the arms swing freely into place. As one arm moves forward, the other moves back (3). The same motion (4) can be performed by stepping forward with the front foot (5) and letting the arms swing freely, just like the first example (6).

Knee Motion

The knee motion that is used in taijutsu can be studied in the following technique. From jumonji no kamae (1), the motion begins in the back knee (2), which will move the entire body back. The motion is completed by pulling forward with the front knee to strike with the forward hand (3).

A practical example of this motion can be seen from the following two techniques. The attack comes from the right hand in the form of a straight punch (1). Without moving his feet, the defender on the left rocks back (2) and blocks the attack (3), then rocks forward (4) to strike into the attacker's underarm.

This same motion can be used even when the attack comes from close range. The attack is a straight punch to the face (1). The defender rocks (2) back to avoid the attack and then rocks forward (3) to strike the attacker's face. He continues forward and sweeps the attacker's front leg upward with his thigh while pushing his head back (4). This action drops the attacker to the ground.

Another basic motion that is important is ukinagashi or receiving flow. From a natural stance (1) one steps back and brings the arms up (2) so that the incoming attack (3) is avoided and one is in a good position to counterattack (4).

Receiving motion is often used and combined with several counterattacks. The defender (1) steps back (2) then delivers a quick hit with the front hand (3). He then steps through to hit with the back hand (4). It should be noted that both of these strikes are done in conjunction with proper knee motion and thus have the entire weight of the body behind them.

An example of receiving flow in application can be seen in the following: The attacker steps in with a straight punch, which is avoided with ukinagashi (1). The defender strikes (2) and steps in with a side of the hand strike ("shuto") to the attacker's neck (3).

The same technique can also be used close in, as illustrated in photos (4, 5 & 6).

When studying the techniques in this book, it should be remembered that these motions are not dead forms and can be applied in a variety of situations. For example (1), the attack is a straight thrust. Instead of stepping back, the defender angles forward so as to catch the attacker's front hand (2). He then steps forward to strike the attacker (3), which drops and disarms him (4).

The use of the hicho no kamae can be seen from the following examples. It should be noted that one does not stop in this stance and just stand on one foot waiting for the opponent to attack. Rather, this stance and all the others are models for proper movement. Stances are one method for training proper movement.

From the doko no kamae, the front leg is brought back and the front hand drops down in a sweeping motion (1) and then upward as the knee raises to kick (2 & 3). As one recovers, the back hand is brought around to strike with a shuto (4).

The use of hicho no kamae in application can be seen in the following example. The attacker (1) lunges with a low body punch (2). This is avoided by the defender who then sweeps the attacker's punching arm up (3) to make an opening for a kick (4). This is followed by a shuto to the neck of the attacker (5). The defender then turns (6) and throws the attacker to the ground (7).

Hicho can also be used against close-range kicks. The attacker on the right tries to kick the defender's groin (1). This attack is blocked and the defender sweeps the attacker's leg away (2) to break his balance. As he steps down (3), the defender strikes the attacker's neck (4).

It should be noted that the hicho motion is very useful in weapons situations. The man with the staff (1) strikes at the swordsman's front leg. The swordsman retreats the leg (2) and brings the sword in position to strike (3) by stepping down inside the reach of the staff (4).

Some of the basic wrestling techniques can be seen in the following examples. Once again, the basic technique is given along with an example of an application.

The first technique is mushadori. From the arm held position (1), step forward and drop the held arm over the opponent's arm (2), entrapping his entire arm (3). Lifting will dislocate the shoulder or throw the attacker over backward (4).

Another practical example of mushadori can be seen in the following sequence. From a double hand grab (1), the defender on the left steps forward and strikes his attacker in the face with his forehead (2). He then turns his body (3) and applies mushadori (4).

The next technique is a basic wrist lock. From a kneeling lapel grab (1), the defender countergrabs the arm (2) and applies a wrist lock/elbow bar (3) to control and drop the attacker (4).

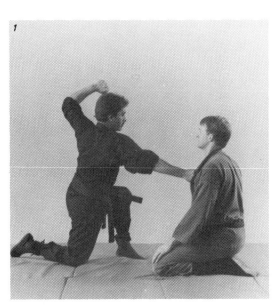

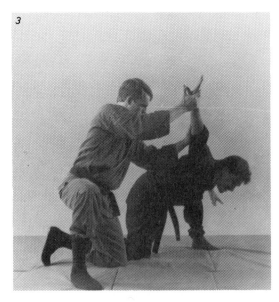

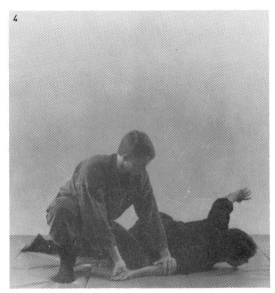

On a more practical level, the first attack (usually a punch or a kick), must be dealt with before a lock or takedown can be applied.

As the attacker hooks a punch at the defender's face (1), the defender steps in and strikes the attacker's collarbone with his forearm to stop the punch (2). He then follows with an elbow strike to the face as he grabs the wrist (3), steps and pivots as he locks (4), and finishes with a takedown. The initial counterblow "softens" up the attacker for the wrestling technique.

The same type of technique can be applied in the other direction — that is, twisting the opponent's wrist to the outside.

Here, the defender handles the grab and punch (1) by stepping in and pinning the wrist against his chest (2) as he twists to the outside and strikes the attacker's face (3). Applying a two-hand wrist lock (4), he steps back and takes down the attacker.

Once again, it is often necessary to deal with the attacker's first technique before resorting to a wrestling hold.

In this example (1), the defender will simultaneously avoid the punch and lock the wrist by pinning it while rolling his left shoulder (like a Western boxer) to slip the punch (2). Continuing the movement (3) throws the attacker down for a knee-assisted wrist lock/arm bar (4).

The next technique is called gansekinaga, and it is the foundation of tai-jutsu throwing skills. Unlike judo or aikido throws, which often make it possible for the thrown person to land safely by using a roll or break-fall, the throwing techniques of taijutsu are performed so that the opponent does not fall so nicely. In fact, the opponent's less-than-ideal landing is more important than how high or how far he is thrown. The advantages of this particular throw are manifold, and if done properly, it is difficult to counter.

Against a grab (1), the thrower steps forward and loops his arm under the attacker's arm (2); note how this begins to unbalance the attacker. Next, the thrower steps inside (3) and turns his body to make the throw work (4).

A practical application of gansekinaga can be seen in the following example. The attacker at the right leads with a kick (1), which is avoided with ukinagashi (2). The defender steps in to strike the attacker's solar plexus. He then slides his hand into position (3), steps in and lifts the arm (4). By twisting his stance (5), the defender completes the throw (6).

Covering Ground

Often it is necessary for a martial artist to cover ground in a hurry because of an opponent's reach advantage with a weapon. Most of the motions used for this type of movement employ some form of cross step.For short distances, the X-step is used (1-3). It works in unarmed situations where one is faced with a fairly short weapon such as a knife or short stick. The X-step is also used when armed with a weapon.

For longer distances, a scissor jump is better. From a ready stance (1), the back leg is thrown forward (2). This pulls the body forward (3). This motion is used to cover more ground than a simple X-step. Lastly, one must be able to move forward while jumping to avoid various attacks to the legs (4-6).

An example of avoiding an attack while closing with the opponent can be seen in the following unarmed vs. bo technique. From long range (1), the attacker uses a sweeping attack at the unarmed man's legs. The defender jumps forward and up to avoid the attack (2) and delivers a double kick to the opponent's body (3).

An example of an application of the scissor jump can be seen in the following: Armed with a bo, the attacker swings at the defender's thigh (1). The defender jumps in behind a scissor jump/kick (2) and slams his shoulder into the attacker's hand (3). Trapping the bo and lead arm, the defender levers him into an arm lock (4) and uses the pole to force him down into a painful submission hold (5-8).

Dropping

Another useful move is that of dropping under an opponent's technique. From a relaxed posture (1), the defender waits for the straight punch, which he avoids by dropping down on one knee (2). It is important to note that the knee lands on top of the attacker's foot, probably breaking it. The defender then slams his shoulder into the attacker's front knee (3). This knocks the opponent onto his back (4). He rolls forward (5) and slams an elbow into the downed opponent (6).

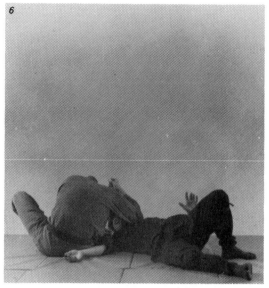

Often the drop can be used after the first attack is avoided. The attacker leads with a straight punch, which is avoided in uki fashion (1). The defender immediately drops to attack the opponent's knee (2), and levers the ankle up (3). Downed, a leg twist (4) is used to turn him over for pinning (5).

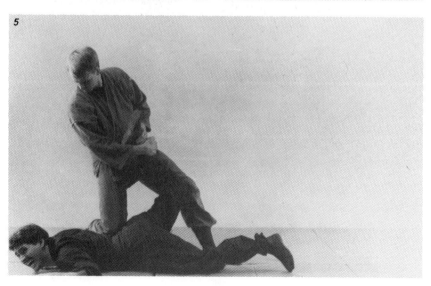

This dropping motion is also very useful when one is faced with an incoming weapon. Here, the attacker cuts at the unarmed man (1), who ducks under the cut and uses a body strike to jam and stun the swordsman (2). He then drives an elbow into the groin (3) and throws him over his back by pulling the sword hands and lifting with his left shoulder (4). As the swordsman lands, the defender grabs his wrist for a lock (5) and holds him in a submission hold. The defender's foot pins the attacker, as does the sword's lethal threat (6), which the defender alertly retrieved.

Rolling

The importance of break-falling and rolling skills are easy to overlook. While it is true that people often go through life without ever being involved in a life-and-death fight, the same cannot be said of simply falling down. The author knows a number of people who have suffered permanent damage to their bodies from what would seem to be fairly harmless falls. Also, if one is not reasonably skilled with these techniques, he simply cannot learn advanced techniques or be involved in any form of rough training. Therefore, these techniques are VERY important, and one can never really learn enough about them.

Rolling should be practiced from all stances in all directions and on a variety of surfaces. In the author's opinion, rolling on ice is a very good method to learn a great deal about these techniques. For the sake of explanation, rolling takes two broad forms. These are nagarei and keiten; that is, drops and diving rolls.

The backward roll can be seen in the following photos. From a ready position (1), the motion starts with a short backward step and drop (2). It is important to note the placement of the left foot, which supports the body drop. The roll is a single smooth motion (3) from hip to opposite shoulder. At the end of the roll (4), one should stand without having to use one's hands.

Another type of roll that is similar but in a different direction is yokonagarei or side flowing roll. From a ready position (1), one drops straight to the ground (2) and rolls over (3 & 4) so as to rise without using one's hands (5).

83

Nagarei should be studied in all possible directions. The straight drop to the inside of the body (1-3) is an important evasion technique.

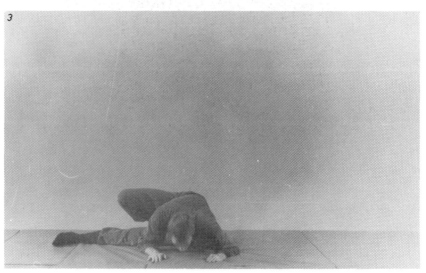

The dropping motion can also be used to upset an opponent's attack. As the attacker steps in with a lunging punch (1), the defender drops straight down to his outside and blocks the incoming leg (2). This will, if timed properly, send the attacker flying because of the forward momentum of his own punch (3).

The straight drop can be combined with a backward rolling motion to follow up a downed opponent. The attacker uses an overhand stabbing attack (1). The defender drops and blocks the attacker's leg as he steps in (2). As the attacker is thrown, the defender grabs the knife hand (3) and continues his backward roll (4) so as to end up on the attacker's back with the knife hand in a wrist lock (5). Sitting up, the defender can apply a submission hold (6).

It should be noted that because of the angle, the defender drops slightly to the side of the line of attack. In this way, the defender is able to control the knife and the attacker lands on the ground, not on top of the defender.

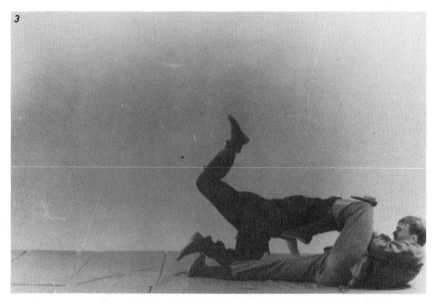

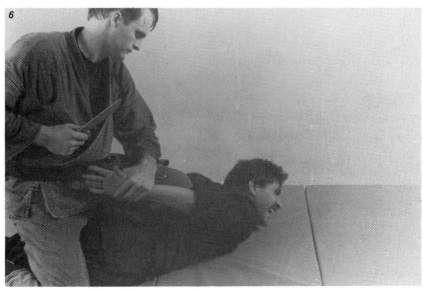

One example of how all the various stages of the nagarei motion can be used can be seen in the following unarmed vs. sword (muto) example. The swordsman attacks with a horizontal (dogiri) cut (1). The defender drops under the cut and at the same time extends one leg upward (2), so that the swordsman slams his own hands into the defender's foot (3). Often this is enough to disarm the attacker. The attack to the hands is followed by a trap of the attacker's front leg (4), and by kicking the knee (5), the defender forces his opponent to the ground (6).

The rolling in taijutsu is also used to escape from an attacker's technique. The attacker on the right uses an outward wrist lock (1). The defender responds by turning slightly and dropping to the ground (2) and rolling backward (3). The force of the roll pulls his hand free (4 & 5).

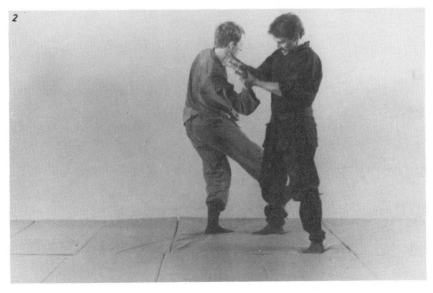

94

A set of techniques that are related to rolling is the variety of handsprings that can also be used to escape from an opponent.

To escape from an arm lock (1), the ninja dives forward (2) and uses a one-hand handspring to free his arm (3 & 4).

These handsprings can be applied in a number of situations where normal break-falls or rolling would not be enough. The attacker on the right steps in (1) and twists (2) to set up a shoulder throw. But as the defender is thrown, he dives forward and performs a one-hand handspring to stop his fall (3), then drops to the ground to pull the opponent forward (4) for a leg lock counter to the head (5, 6 & 7).

There are, of course, many ways to deal with a throwing attack, many of which do not require acrobactic ability. In this technique, the attacker steps in for a hip throw (1), but the defender counters by checking the hip (2) and stepping behind (3) for his own hip throw (4, 5 & 6) and armbar (7).

The diving type of roll is used when one needs to reach the ground head first. This is often necessary if one wishes to cover a greater distance than is possible with a drop or roll. These dives should be practiced by beginning with kneeling rolls and gradually working into rolls from a standing position. Later, rolling without placing one's hands on the ground and long diving rolls are practiced. It is also good to train rolling while holding a weapon and on icy surfaces, such as frozen lakes.

The standard side roll or "yoko keiten" begins from a natural posture (1), knees bent. One dives out (not down) to the side and rolls across the back (2, 3 & 4), coming up into a raised posture ready to stand or roll again (5). Never take your eyes off your opponent while rolling.

The forward roll is called "zenpo keiten." Begin in a natural posture with one foot forward (1), and using your arm and back like a wheel (2 & 3), roll diagonally across the back. Come up without using your hands (4). It is very helpful if one exhales as he performs all rolling and dropping motions.

Dive rolls are particularly useful for escaping attacks. Confronted with a sword-wielding opponent (1), the ninja waits for him to attack (2) and then rolls away at the last instant (3 & 4).

The unarmed defender can run away, throw shuriken or a handful of dirt into the attacker's face, or simply pause to see what will happen next.

Rolling can be used for both offense and defense. This is particularly the case if one is confronted with a long weapon and is unarmed. Against a staff-armed opponent (1), the ninja rolls under the opponent's sideward blow (2 & 3) to close in and deliver a kick to the attacker's midsection (4).

Although not practiced often, this type of rolling can be used against a high kicker's base leg. If one does practice this technique, a word of warning is necessary because this technique has a tendency to do some rather heavy damage — even when done slowly. A basic example would be a high side kick (1 & 2), which the ninja avoids by using a ducking motion (3). He then springs forward under the kicker's leg (4) and rolls forward on the attacker's base leg (5 & 6) and finishes the struggle with a headlock pin (7).

Like all well-rounded martial arts, taijutsu deals with a variety of unexpected attacks. The following two examples show how a grabbing attack from behind can be dealt with.

Against a bear hug (1), the defender drops his body weight (2) and reaches through his own legs to grab the leg of the attacker (3). The defender then leans back and sits on the attacker's leg, forcing him to the ground (4).

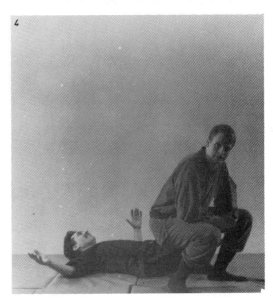

Again against a bear hug attack (1), the defender hits back with his hips and raises his elbows as he strikes with the back of his head (2). This loosens the attacker's grip, and the defender is able to grab the hands (3) and whip him to the ground (4 & 5). Once down, the defender turns him over (6 & 7) and pins him (8).

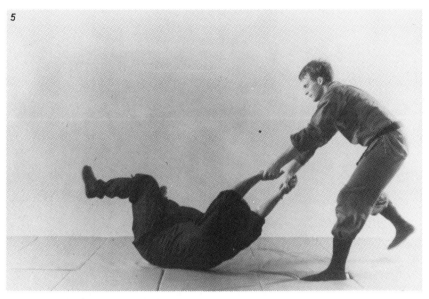

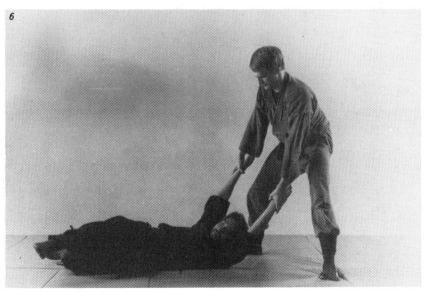

115

Taijutsu makes judicious use of kicking techniques. The kicks themselves are fairly simple in nature, avoiding the loss of balance often caused by fancier but no more powerful kicks. It should be noted that the kicks used in taijutsu are slammed into place so as to knock the opponent down or back. This is very different from the snap kicks used in many styles of karate or kung-fu. Part of this may have to do with the use of armor by some of the ninja's historical opponents. However, it is more likely that the slamming type of kicks are more natural movements than snapping kicks. The type of kicks used in taijutsu do not lead to the joint injuries of the legs often seen in sport martial arts.

One of the simplest and most powerful kicks of taijutsu is the heel stomp kick. The back leg (1) is brought up (2) so that the knee touches the shoulder (3). The leg then shoots forward so that the target is struck with the heel (4). The kicker then steps down to finish the kick (5). In reality, this kick works much like a giant walking step.

The same kick can be used somewhat like a forward snap kick so that the back leg is pulled forward (6 & 7) and then shot straight into the target (8). This kick is effective when used against the lower targets on an attacker's body.

Often, kicks are used to counter kicking attacks. This is because the distance covered by a kick is greater than that of a punch, and therefore, the defender is further away before he begins his counter. For example, the attacker on the right initiates a straight kick (1 & 2), which the defender deflects (3 & 4). As the attacker's leg drops (a natural reaction to the deflection), the defender rocks forward (5) and stomp kicks to the attacker's ribs (6).

To block or deflect a low kick, the arch of the foot or shin can be used effectively. Here are two examples:

The attacker on the right aims a low kick at the knee (1). The defender catches the ankle with his rear foot, stopping the kick's momentum (2), and counters by kicking to the attacker's groin in the same motion (3).

In the second example, the defender sidesteps (4), catches the kick with his raised shin (5) and pushes the leg away (6). The defender follows up with a grab (7) and strike to the head (8).

125

7

8

126

Muto: Unarmed Against a Weapon

The practice of "muto" or no sword is very important in taijutsu. Muto really means the art of defending oneself regardless of the situation. All too often, one joins a particular school and becomes restricted to that style, thus becoming confused when confronted with the unexpected. It should be remembered that muto does not mean always taking the opponent's weapon, but rather not losing to the opponent's (being struck) weapon. Obviously, if one is skilled in this area then weapon vs. weapon should not be a big problem.

The timing of this type of training is the point; one should move at the last moment. A simple but effective training drill is shown in the following series. From a natural posture (1), as the attacker steps in (2), the defender waits until the last moment, then steps away from the cut (3). One should be careful with the placement of his hands.

The type of timing used and developed through such training makes it possible to throw an attacker with a minimum of effort. In the following example, a lunging punch (4 & 5) is countered by a sidestep and a pull to the attacking hand (6). If timed correctly, this motion will send the attacker flying (7).

The number of techniques that are used when unarmed against weapons is limitless. A number of examples can be given to show that many ideas and motions can be used in a variety of circumstances. The "taiken" or body strike is often used in such situations. This is a very high-level technique because to be performed properly, the defender must put his body in the exact place the attacker's body is supposed to go.

The (1) swordsman uses a horizontal (dogiri) cut, which the defender counters by stepping straight in (2), thereby letting the attacker's hands smash into his shoulder (3). The defender then turns (4) and throws the attacker to the ground (5).

Stepping inside an arching attack is often used in taijutsu. Facing an Iai type attack (1) the defender steps inside the arch of the draw and controls the attacker's arm (2). A strike to the ribs (3) sets the swordsman up for an arm bar (4), takedown (5), shoulder lock (6 & 7).

135

The relationship of unarmed techniques and unarmed vs. weapon techniques can be seen in the following: Uki nagashi and a kick are used to deal with a straight punching attack (1-3). When faced with a sword, the same type of movement can be used. As the attacker cuts downward (4), the defender sidesteps forward and punches the swordsman's arm (5) and kicks upward into his forearms (6) to disarm him. As he steps down, the defender catches one arm (7) and drops the opponent with an arm lock (8).

139

The body turn (1-3) is very important for dealing with thrusting weapon attacks; that is, any type of attack that comes in a straight line at the defender. Here, the attack is a forward thrust (4), which the defender avoids by pivoting (5). Note that the swordsman's hand is also caught in the same motion. The defender then places his hand on the back of the sword and rocks forward (6) to cut the attacker with his own sword (7).

The same pivoting motion can be incorporated into a forward stepping motion to close with an opponent who is farther away. The attacker uses a straight thrust (1), which is avoided by a step and pivot (2). The step is necessary because of the reach advantage of the bo. The defender then steps in and pulls (3) the boman in and down (4), and finishes with a disarm and pin (5 & 6).

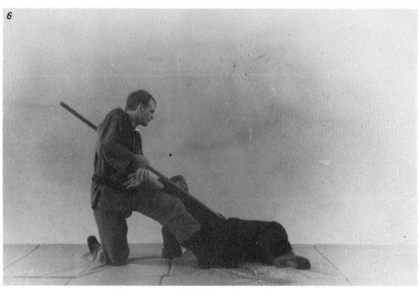

Although not always the most recommended action, it is possible to grab a sword by the blade. This is usually done when the defender avoids a cut but is not close enough to the swordsman to trap a hand. The swordsman attacks with an overhead strike (menuchi) (1), which is avoided (2) by pivoting. As the sword stroke is stopped, the defender grabs it (3) and uses a knee attack (4) to twist the sword out of the opponent's hand (5).

The ability to deal with multiple attacks is also studied in taijutsu. Grabbed by two opponents (1), the ninja steps forward and folds his elbows in (2). He then rocks back and loops his arms over to unbalance both attackers (3), which drop them (4). From this point, the ninja can deal with his attacker or simply run away (5).

Often one is held by an assailant while being attacked by another. The ninja waits for the attack to come (1), then drops (2 & 3) so that the attacker strikes his assistant (4). The swordsman is then dealt with by striking to a nerve center (5).

153

UNIQUE LITERARY BOOKS OF THE WORLD

Also publishers of:
Inside Karate
Inside Kung-Fu

UNIQUE PUBLICATIONS
4201 Vanowen Place
Burbank, CA 91505

PLEASE WRITE IN
FOR OUR LATEST CATALOG